D1566925

Dedicated to

Leo James McNevin

You shine brighter than the Moon

Somervillage Books
Richmond, Virginia

Walking with the Moon

A Mindfulness Walk

by Christy Somerville

Illustrations by Jim Somerville

I roll out of bed,

My feet hit the floor,

I name three things

I am thankful for.

The world is so busy,

I need to slow down,

To open my eyes

And look all around.

I put on my shoes

And head out the door,

I'm ready to ramble

And look for some more.

When, Oh! There's the Moon!

So big and so bright,

He shines in the sky

Like a big flashlight!

Come on, Moon!

I'll show you the way.

A wonderful way

To start a new day.

Walk with your senses—

Sound, smell, and sight—

These are the things

That will start your day right.

I see a puppy,

With fluffy, soft fur.

Her human seems happy

To take care of her.

I walk and I walk

On the leaves near the street,

Hearing the crunching sound

Under my feet.

The church on the corner

Is covered in lights;

Their glow spreads its warmth

On a cold, dark night.

I rub the green leaves

Of a lavender bush,

The scent calms my mind,

And slows down the rush.

Neon gloves
And a hat so bright,
A man jogs by
In the pale moonlight.

Walk with me, Moon;

There's still more to see!

Beautiful things

Are all around me!

I pass the museum

With a man on a horse,

Wow, Mr. Moon,

He's a powerful force!

I pass the big houses

With colorful lights

My mind wakes up

To a world of delight.

The ginkgo leaves

Are gold in the glow

The streetlights make them

Quite the show!

The full moon hides

And reappears,

It's like a game

As he draws near.

Is that you, Moon?

I touch the bark

Of my favorite tree,

Full of thanksgiving

For all that I see.

I breathe in the love,

The joy and the glad;

I breathe out the fear,

The worry and mad.

I hear the sparrow's

Cheerful song,

It quickens my step

And moves me along.

Come on, Moon!

Come walk with me.

Let's look at the mural

Of flowers and bees.

I'm almost home

And the day's getting lighter,

The moon's hard to see,

The sky's getting brighter.

I'm using my senses,

But what can I taste?

Maybe a smoothie

From this little place!

My walk's almost over

A hundred yards more,

I brush by the flag

At the market's front door.

With gratitude

And joy in my heart,

I'm feeling much better,

A great way to start!

The sign in the window's

A perfect reminder.

I try to be kind...

...But today I'll be kinder.

Made in the USA
Columbia, SC
01 March 2021